I0075095

volum**1**

T.J. Rohleder Presents...

THE BLACK BOOK OF MARKETING SECRETS

The Best Ideas from the Powerful
RUTHLESS MARKETING Program!

Copyright ® MMVII by M.O.R.E. Incorporated.

All rights reserved. No part of this book may be used
or reproduced in any manner whatsoever without
written permission except in the case of brief
quotations embodied in critical articles and reviews.
For information address: M.O.R.E. Incorporated,
305 East Main Street, Goessel, Kansas 67053-0198.

FIRST EDITION

ISBN-10: 1-933356-12-X
ISBN-13: 978-1-933356-12-9

Edited & Designed by Chris Bergquist

Printed in the United States of America

Dear Friend,

I absolutely love marketing! I love to think about it, write about it, and talk about it. I love to find all kinds of ways to use it to build my businesses. This is such a fascinating subject! Whoever said that "marketing takes a day to learn and lifetime to master" was right!

For years I have been keeping journals that are filled with the best marketing ideas. Now I am happy to share some of my favorite ideas with you.

Here is the first volume of some of the best marketing ideas I've found and know to be true. If you like what you read – please go to my website and discover how much more great information I have for you! Enjoy!

Sincerely,

T.J. Rohleder
Co-Founder of M.O.R.E. Incorporated

What are the 3 BIGGEST THINGS your customers <u>want</u> – and how can you give it to them?

a. Find the best answer to that question...

b. Tweak it – work with it – refine it – polish it...

c. Then shout it as loudly as you can!!!

Let the people in your market hear it in the <u>clearest</u> and <u>most</u> <u>compelling</u> <u>way</u>!

THE **BLACK** BOOK OF MARKETING SECRETS volume **1**
Go to RuthlessMarketing.com/freegift Now to Get a FREE Gift!

1

THOUGHT JOGGERS:

> What are your top five greatest selling messages?

> Why should they buy from <u>YOU</u> and not someone else?

> What are the strongest inducements that will make them buy right now?
  - *The best offer?*
  - *The best bribe?*

> What is the <u>strongest</u> <u>and</u> <u>most</u> <u>believable</u> reason to get them to send you their money right away?

Your intimate understanding of your market and core business is the #1 ingredient for riches.

The more you know about the customer...

    a. What they have bought before – or are buying now.
    b. Their problems, frustration, pain, hopes, and dreams.
    c. And how your product – service – company can offer them a solution to "B" – the more effective you can be at selling them.

Knowing MORE about your customer lets you MAXIMIZE the up-sell.

FOCUS

Focus on the areas you are best in – and those that bring you the most money.

Find your small niche – and EXPLOIT THE HELL out of it!

How do you get the biggest BANG for your BUCK?

1. Spend <u>more</u> <u>money</u> to reach <u>less</u>, but better qualified prospects.

2. Focus more time on re-selling <u>to</u> <u>your</u> <u>best</u> <u>customers</u>!

EMOTIONS

Never forget that you are always selling to people's self-centered emotions...

People buy for emotional reasons:

- Greed
- Guilt
- Fear
- Pride
- Love

We are all self-centered people living in a totally self-centered world!

Constantly flow your cash back into the areas of your marketing that made you the most money to begin with.

You can't re-invent the wheel – but you must make it "seem" as if you have!!

The very best way to get someone to give you $3,000.00 is to <u>first</u> get them to give you $300.00!

Marketing skills are improved and even mastered with knowledge, practice – and years of experience.

Copy shamelessly.

Focus on your core business.

The market comes first.

Formula:

a. Get the right message or offer.
b. To the right market.
c. Through the right media.

Direct Response Marketing is a personal medium:

- Write and speak <u>to</u> <u>only</u> <u>one</u> <u>person</u>.
- The art is to make the person you are communicating with seem special.
- The more you can make them feel you are <u>only</u> <u>speaking</u> <u>to</u> <u>them</u> – the better.

W.I.F.M.

Strive to answer the question:

"What's in it for me?"

MARKETING

Marketing is all the activities, plans, schemes, and ideas that let you:

    a. Attract and sell to <u>new</u> customers...

    b. And then continue re-selling to your <u>old</u> customers.

Within these two simple steps are about 100 million subtle variations of what you can do to be most effective.

Use <u>plain</u> – <u>direct</u>
– <u>simple</u> – and
FORCEFUL
writing that goes
<u>straight</u> to the
emotions of
your reader.

The truth is 100-times
stronger than a lie!

USE IT!

Honesty cuts!

It cuts into the clutter
of all the other marketing
messages that are also
after your target market.

Work ON it – not IN it.

Be the architect of your business – <u>not</u> the worker or foreman. Definition: The architect designs the building – and sees to it that his plans are followed by the builders. The same is true in business. We must design successful marketing systems – and then monitor them closely.

The best ideas come to you in the heat of the moment!

Write down your best ideas when they are new – and when you are first getting started and very excited!

- <u>These</u> <u>ideas</u> <u>are</u> <u>HOT</u>! You'll need them later on when you are cold!!!
- Ideas are like slippery fish! Hard to hold onto! So you must capture them fast!

The Slack Adjuster –

Develop and promote at least one super high-profit item that helps to build your overall net profits.

- This is crucial. You must develop this super high-profit margin to make up for all of the high expenses that eat into your profit margins.

Prepare for the worst possible outcomes – So you can still make money with terrible numbers.

- Set your margins high.
- Factor in low response rates.
- Figure out how to make the promotion work – even if the numbers are bad.

"Believability Is More Important Than Credibility."

Dan Kennedy

Dan's Analogy: Bill Clinton – a known liar, but comes across as believable!

How Can You Build More Believability Into Your Promotions?

The **BIG** Promise

At the core of every great promotion – or marketing message is – The BIG Promise!

- Make it BIGGER!
- Match it to your market...
- And you'll make millions!

Formula...

a. Discover and Create the biggest and most compelling promise
b. Find as many different ways to "say" or communicate this promise
c. Weave all these different ways into your promotion.

Keep re-slamming them with your biggest promises!

There are only 3 ways to build a business:

1. Get more customers.

2. Sell more high-ticket items – for bigger profits.

3. Sell more often to your customers!

Almost all million-dollar marketing ideas are transferable from one business to another.

5 Elements Of Every Super-Successful Direct-Response Message:

1. Meaningful specifics – <u>not</u> vague generalities.
2. A promise.
3. An offer or offers.
4. Precise commands – *"Here's what I want you to do now."*
5. An extra reason to act immediately.

Dan Kennedy

$ $ $ $ $

Customers in all markets
want someone to do
<u>everything</u> for them.

$ $ $ $ $

You must sell people the
things they want – <u>NOT</u> the
things you want to sell them!

* *It's all about them, not you.*

$ $ $ $ $

"Empathy" is a very important asset of any marketing campaign.

- You must speak directly to their heart... straight to their self-centered emotions!

Become an expert at getting inside the minds and hearts of your best prospects and customers.

Think in concepts.

See what others can't see – or overlook.

Overview of a successful marketing campaign –

    a. Take the best sales points and "schemes" that have worked before…

    b. Find new ways to hook them together… new themes, new angles

    c. Then smooth it out… So it sounds new and different.

Keep finding ways
to re-invent the greatest
themes – ideas – and
powerful selling messages
that have worked like
gangbusters before.

The 5 emotional reasons that people buy anything and everything:

- Pride: Desire to be better than others... POWER.
- Love.
- Fear.
- Greed.
- Guilt.

Every reason to buy can be linked back to these 5 powerful emotional factors.

Selling is finding out what people want - and letting them have it!

$ $ $ $ $

Nobody wants a business –
they only want what
they perceive a business
can give to them.

- Same with any other product. People buy the perceived benefits.

- They buy for the emotional things they perceive they'll receive.

Your business is very similar to a living organism...

- The marketplace is its life and livelihood.

- It feeds off its market.

- It changes, grows, and adapts to the changes in its environment.

- Many outside forces can kill it. Some slowly. Some quickly.

- Keeping it alive for a long time can be a delicate thing.

Timing is vital. You have to get it while it's HOT!

It's not...

> *"Let's make as much money as we can as fast as we can..."*

It's....

> *"Let's make money fast – while we can!"*

Markets change fast – what's hot today can be cold tomorrow.

Follow the Leader...

- Who are the biggest and most successful companies in your market?

- What are they doing?

- How can you model after them as closely as possible?

Match them closely first.

Then figure out the subtle differences you can exploit.

Your BIGGEST profits will always come from the back-end...

- Spend more time – money – and effort – doing more business with your existing customers.

- 20% of your marketing should be aimed at getting new customers.

- 80% of your marketing should go towards doing more business with your existing customers.

Forget all the complicated MBA crap! Getting rich in your own business is pretty damn simple (not easy)...

Here's the formula:

1. Just get a large enough number of people...

2. To consistently give you a large enough amount of money...

3. At a large enough profit margin per transaction...

And you will get rich!

Build strong bonds of loyalty with your customers.

This relationship is worth its weight in gold!

Test new ideas and promotions to your best customers first.

If it doesn't work to that group – it won't work to the other prospects you have no relationship with.

The very act of buying something satisfies many people's desires to gain the benefits of your product or service.

- It makes them feel good about themselves.

- It makes them "feel" they are doing something positive.

- It satisfies their emotional desires.

The best selling messages – and offers grow and develop as you work on them.

- You must take the leap of faith – and develop it gradually as you go.

- Whatever you focus on expands! So keep focusing on improving each offer.

- More often than not, your best ideas will come as the deadline approaches!

Selling is the art of proving that what you have to offer is worth far, far MORE than the money they must give up.

Emergency money-making generator...

When times get hard...

When business gets slow...

When you need cash-flow to feed the monster...

<u>All</u> <u>you</u> <u>do</u> <u>is</u>:

a. Go to your best customers...

b. Make them an irresistible offer they can't refuse!

c. Have a special sale that will blow them away!

Do this and they'll stand in line with money in hand!

A famous marketing guru said that the secret to writing a powerful sales letter is to imagine that someone has a gun to your head the entire time you're writing – and you must sell everyone you are writing to – or you'll get killed!

Keep the pressure on!

Set out to do <u>more</u> than you think you can do.

Set tighter deadlines – and always have your next job waiting in the wings.

Wisdom comes from getting your ass kicked by the brutal realities of life.

- You get the shit kicked out of you – then you heal and become stronger.

Any fool can make money in a good market – when everything is working in their favor.

- But when markets change or dry up – that's when you come face-to-face with the brutal reality of business.

- That's when you learn all of the really great lessons.

U.S.P.

The goal of developing the perfect Unique Selling Position is to be <u>different from the rest</u>!

- Different in some way that is very important to the core group of customers you serve.

Being different will separate your company from all the nameless/faceless "me too" competitors in your market.

"Good Marketing Is A Combination Of Fishing And Chess!"

Eric Bechtold

All great fishermen know that the true secret to catching the big ones is:

1. Use the right bait.

2. Think like the fish!

3. <u>Never</u> reveal the hook.

All fishermen for sales and profits should pay attention!!

Your Marketing System Can Make You Super Rich.

The purpose of a good marketing system is to bring you a steady flow of qualified prospects... who want what you offer.

- They come to you pre-sold!

- Converting large numbers of these prospects to sales is now even easier.

Great marketing has a lot in common with religion...

- The story must be emotional – simple – positive – and compelling.

- It must make BIG promises – salvation now! Not later!

- It must offer hope.

- It must appeal to the two main emotions: <u>greed</u> <u>and</u> <u>fear</u>.

- It must promise people the opportunity to rise above others and be superior to them.

That's the BIG one! Everyone wants to be superior...

"Genius is 99% perspiration – and 1% inspiration."

Albert Einstein

Developing great selling messages is a process – not an event!

- You must flush-out the best selling and marketing ideas.

- The best ideas develop after a great amount of brainstorming and work.

- It takes a lot of time, work, thinking, and re-thinking.

3 BIG promises that hook people:

1. You can offer them products and services that give them the thing(s) they desire.

2. You offer them a justification for all their failures. (This makes them feel good about themselves.)

3. You promise them an endless future supply of <u>even</u> <u>more</u> of the things they want!

2-Step Marketing is the safest and most profitable way to make money.

Step One: Attract a highly qualified prospect.

- Use a great offer.
- Don't try to sell them too much at first.
- Get your hooks into them.
- Make it as easy as possible for them to buy the first time.
- Sell a low-priced widget.
- Educate them.
- Make them feel that *"They came to you"* – and <u>not</u> the other way around.

Step Two: SLAM THEM!

- Now bring out the BIG GUNS!
- You already have their attention and interest… Now you are in the position to show them how you can give them what they desire.

People want "The MAGIC Bullet!"

- The one product/service that is going to make everything okay.

- It's going to quickly solve some major problem.

- Or provide them with a miracle cure!

- Or an instant solution!

If they believe you can give these things to them – you'll get more people to quickly give you more money.

Marketing Questions:

1. Who do you want to reach?

2. What bait will we use to attract and then sell them?

   The "Bait" is the offer and entire theme behind the promotion.

   a. The market comes first. (Who do you want?)

   b. Then comes the bigger question – attracting – selling and re-selling them.

   c. Answer this question:

      "Why should I (your prospect) choose to do business with you – versus any and every other option available to me in your category?"
      Dan Kennedy

Marketing is simply a 3-step process:

1. Attracting qualified leads.

2. Converting the highest percentage possible into first-time sales.

3. Re-selling the largest number of customers, as many times as you can, for the highest profit from each sale.

These are the only 3 steps! However, each one must be done the right way.

MARKETING MAXIM:

You can tell everything about a person – by simply paying attention to what they spend their money on.

- People reveal their true selves – by the way they spend their money.

- Especially their disposable income.

- "It is where a man spends his money that shows where his heart lies."
  A. Edwin Keigurn

- This is why 2-step marketing is so powerful.

Get them to jump through hoops to qualify themselves.

> You get them to show their level of interest by taking a specific action.

> The bigger the action they must take – the more they reveal how interested and serious they are.

Now you use this knowledge to sell the hell out of them!

Hype Sells!

Don't be afraid to use the power of hype:

- People want it!

- It stirs their emotions – and pumps them up!

- You now have their full attention – you have broken through the clutter.

Of course, the art is using hype – <u>without</u> making it sound like hype!

4 stages of learning anything new:

1. **Unconscious Incompetence:**
   You don't know what you don't know! Total Ignorance!

2. **Conscious Incompetence:**
   You begin to realize and discover the things you don't know. This is the frustration and confusion period. You're *still* incompetent... But, at least your eyes are beginning to open.

3. **Conscious Competence:**
   You can function in the new area – but, it's a major struggle – and you're not very good.

4. **Unconscious Competence:**
   MASTERY! You have mastered the main areas and you do it naturally – like a duck in the water!

Great Quotes:

"People are silently begging to be led."
> Jay Abraham

"You can learn more from movement than meditation."
> Gary Halbert

"It doesn't have to be good – just good enough."
> Dan Kennedy

"All it takes is just one idea to make a million dollars!"
> Russ von Hoelscher

"We sell to creatures of emotion – bristling with prejudice – and motivated by pride and vanity."
> Dale Carnegie

Direct Response Marketing cuts through the clutter of other advertising – because of one main factor:

It is personal.

- Good D.R.M. is one person communicating with another.

- It is one-to-one communication.

- One beating heart – communicating to another beating heart.

- It doesn't shout – nearly as much as it seductively pulls you in – just like a friendly conversation between two people who care for each other.

The 3-Phase Marketing System that never fails:

- Work your ass off – to create and develop the greatest ads and other sales material – and marketing systems for selling the most products/services for the largest profits.

- Then move forward slowly... Test carefully... Through this process you discover what works best.

- Then put all of your resources into what works best – and test new ideas as you go!

Keep using this system to answer the basic question:

"How high is high?"

THE HAND

Every offer or promotion must meet these five crucial steps:

1. Is it the right offer?

2. Is it going to the right person?

3. Through the right media?

4. With the right hook?

5. And does it fit together with some kind of long-term plan?

There are only a handful – but they're vital. This lets you focus on the essentials.

(I borrowed this hand concept from Bill Graham, the greatest rock-n-roll promoter who ever lived! Bill had his 'handful' of ideas he used for every major event. This let him do BIG THINGS and make quick decisions. It will do the same for you, too!)

Build "risk reversal" into every offer.

- Risk Reversal is taking all the pressure away from the prospect or customer...

- It's an irresistible guarantee.

- It's a dramatic promise that they must gain a major benefit – or they not only get their money back – but they will also receive something of tremendous value!

This blows them away – and will get you a lot of attention and interest.

Every great business and marketing project is put together gradually. ## IT'S A PROCESS.

The Secret:

1. Have a great plan.

2. Focus on what has to be done now and do a little bit every single day.

3. Cross your bridges as you get to them.

It starts with a solid direction – and good plan.

Then it takes a lot of focus and the discipline of consistent effort.

Every prospect we seek is running around with a big sign around their neck that is flashing this message:

"Please make me feel important! And good about myself!"

However, only those with trained eyes can see this sign.

Fulfill the strong desire people have to feel...

- Important
- Esteemed
- Admired
- Beloved
- Special
- Observed

And they will give you everything they have!

Creativity

The creative process is <u>not</u> neat, clean, or pretty. It is not organized. It is dirty, messy, disorganized, and chaotic! It is filled with taking all kinds of unrelated ideas – and <u>mixing</u> <u>them</u> together in a very special way. It is deciding to do something – <u>without</u> knowing how you are going to do it. And then figuring it out as you go!

The Power of Focus:

- Top bull riders are taught to think of nothing except the ride.

- Race car drivers all know that the key is to focus on nothing but their desire to win and the road ahead.

- As entrepreneurs – our focus must be on building our businesses – and creating more sales and profits. Nothing else matters.

How to write a powerful hard-hitting sales letter:

1. Start with a big promise.

2. Paint the picture.

3. Give them proof.

4. Tell them <u>why</u> it's unique.

5. Close your argument by telling them why they must act now!

6. Make them a very special offer <u>if</u> they respond now!

7. End with a reminder of the promise – summary of offer – and STRONG call for action!

That's it! This is the blueprint or schematic of a sales letter – from start to finish.

MASTERY

You do not become a
MASTER by learning
how to do 4,000 things...
You become a MASTER
by doing 12 important
things 4,000 times!

The true art of selling is to sell the concept – not the product or service.

- We sell concepts and solutions.
- We fulfill desires.
- We sell images, dreams, blue sky, hope for the future.
- We sell all things great and imagined that our prospect is longing for.
- We sell to people's greed for more... To their lust... To all their desires... By showing them how our items can somehow give them what they want the most!

And all people want the same basic things...

To feel important...
To feel loved and protected...
To feel safe...
To feel good about themselves.

Test <u>wild</u> <u>new</u> <u>creative</u> <u>ideas</u> <u>slowly</u>. Remember, many of the pioneers got scalped!

> The secret is to make the old stuff look new!

> Keep offering your customers more of whatever they bought from you the first time.

> You simply re-package the same old proven profit making stuff – and give it a whole new gold-plated look and feel.

Selling is the game of understanding people on a very deep level – their fears, hopes, and desires... And then using that knowledge to craft sales messages that go right to the heart and soul of the prospect.

$ $ $ $ $

Develop the killer instinct to go for the money like a wild dog goes <u>straight</u> for the throat!

Good marketing is like war –

- Strike Hard!
- Strike Fast!
- Strike Often!
- Attack!
- Keep hitting them until you get every last dollar you can get from them! The war is won when you get all their money!

When you get a new customer – you <u>must</u> strike FAST – strike HARD – and strike OFTEN!

We use hype and powerful promises for one reason:

To cut through the clutter of the thousands of advertising messages that are begging for our prospects and customers attention every single day.

- People are tuned out.
- They have created a tremendous resistance against ALL sales pitches.
- You have to do something dramatic to wake them up!
- You have to break through their zombie-like fog before you can pitch them.

The only way to do this is to be as dramatic as possible.

The average business person
spends their day "putting out
brush fires"… Their time
and energy gets zapped by all
the minor problems that come
up from day to day. They are
<u>never</u> able to pull back and
work on their businesses.

**There is no real game plan
or strategy!**

Many people think they are
running their companies – but
all they are doing is running
the day-to-day operations…

They are locked into survival.

Creativity comes from __the__ __labor__ of a driven person!

- The harder you work...
- The more you sweat...
- The more you obsess about a specific idea...
- The better your creative ideas will be!

Creativity is finding new ways to solve problems. It's like putting a jigsaw puzzle together... You take all kinds of different pieces – and see how you can fit them together in a new way.

* * * * *

The best ideas are always an expansion and combination of previous ideas that worked.

* * * * *

OPERATION MONEY SUCK:

Invest <u>all</u> of your time, energy, and focus on all the various ways and means of sucking the maximum amount of money from your market.

99% of the focus should be on increasing your sales and profits. This is the life-blood of your business.

No business ever went under for having too many sales and profits!

Look for things that are HOT!

"Whatever is current creates currency."

STEP ONE:
Find people to
sell shit to.

STEP TWO:
Find shit to sell
to those people!

THE BLACK BOOK OF MARKETING SECRETS

Go to RuthlessMarketing.com/freegift Now to Get a FREE Gift!

volume **1**

Selling is like the ritual of dating – the more you need them – the faster they run.

You <u>must</u> <u>let</u> <u>them</u> <u>come</u> <u>to</u> <u>you</u>. The prospect or customer must "feel" that they need <u>you</u> more than you need them.

Your intimate understanding
of your market and core
business is the #1
ingredient for riches.
The more you know
about the customer:

a. What they have bought
   before – or are buying.
b. Their problems,
   frustration, pain.
c. And how your product –
   service – company can
   offer them a solution to
   "B" the more effective you
   can be at selling them.

Strategic thinking is vital to your success in business. And you can't think strategically when you are in the trenches with your troops!

- You must think of yourself as a general in war!

Roll-Out To Mega Wealth!

The same strategy that generated $1,000.00 can be rolled-out to generate $100,000.00 **if** the market is big enough – and other factors can be closely matched.

CREATE *IRRESISTABLE* OFFERS!

"I want to create offers that are like heads of fresh lettuce that are thrown into a pen of starving rabbits!"
(I wrote this in 1997.)

Think on paper!

The very act of putting your ideas on paper forces you to think!

You discover your **BIGGEST** **BREAKTHROUGHS** as you are in the heat of the project!

(Or while working hard on another stressful project.)

Focus on your strengths and make sure you have enough reliable people and systems in place to cover your weaknesses.

There is *so much joy* that comes from the long-term effects of a life of hard work, discipline, focus, goal setting, commitment, and daily striving to work towards your dream.

Commitment/Consistency

Get the prospect to take small, easy baby
steps. Each small step makes it easier for
them to take a bigger step.

- The smaller steps (such as getting
  them to pick up the phone or send for
  something) are the bait that lures
  them into the BIGGER STEPS you
  want them to take.
- And each small commitment they
  make by taking the action you've
  requested strengthens your BOND
  with them.
- Small commitments lead to big
  commitments... Just like a series of
  small actions can lead to powerful habits
  that are almost impossible to break.
- Consistency is re-selling each
  customer the same way all the time.
  People become comfortable with
  certain sales pitches or methods of
  being sold.

The <u>names</u> and <u>addresses</u>
of your best customers
and their past buying
information can be worth
it's weight in diamonds!

*If you know what
to do with this list!*

You increase the demand by adding to the perceived value of all your offers.

You must come up with very solid and believable reasons <u>WHY</u> your offers are limited.

1. Make them believe the value.
2. Make them believe the limited availability.
3. Make them believe the deadline.

Keep giving your customers the same stuff you gave them before – <u>but with a new twist added to it!</u>

The sales copy that worked well once <u>will continue</u> to pull in orders like a money magnet!

---

* * * * *

Blur the lines between your work and play.

* * * * *

Position Yourself As The Expert!

People want to do business with experts. They want to give their money to an expert – *so why not become one?*

View the impossible as just another marketing opportunity!

- Believe so deeply in your ability to give your market what they truly want – that failure is <u>not</u> an option! Develop a missionary zeal for what you do!
- **Then communicate your intense passion to your prospects!**

Find the gaps in your marketplace – and start hammering your wedges into them!

Every market has gaps...
but you'll only find them
by relentless searching.

It's sad, but true. Most people are afraid to write. Years of formal education in the principles of correct usage of the English language has scared them!

<u>Don't let this happen to you.</u> *Remember,* the best English teachers in the world can't sell their way out of a paper bag!

Great Marketers
Are Hunters.

We are happiest when we're on the hunt. The bigger the hunt – the happier we are. *We must be reaching all the time.* All is well as long as our reach exceeds our grasp.

The Secret of Self-Promotion: You are who you say you are!

Direct Mail Marketing is really "Stealth Marketing." *You are flying under the radar!*

None of your competitors ever really know exactly what you're doing! This is <u>a</u> <u>smarter</u> <u>way</u> to do business.

Learning is a process – not an event!

- All skills must be learned. Education can be a slow and painful process. You can increase your knowledge through books and thinking. But there is no substitute for hands-on experience.
- You have to get out there and do it!

The secret of lead generation: You are now a welcomed guest – <u>not</u> an annoying pest!

- √ They sought you out. They are the ones who came to you! You did not go to them!
- √ This difference in positioning is <u>everything</u>. It makes them interested, open, and responsive to your sales message.
- √ **Remember, people like to buy – but they hate being sold. Using lead generation makes them feel in control.**

FREE GIFT!

The ideas in this booklet came from a very special program called:

"RUTHLESS MARKETING ATTACK!"

This is a powerful audio program that reveals 879 of the most aggressive marketing tips, tricks, and strategies you can use to destroy your competition.

If you have enjoyed this booklet, you owe it to yourself to find out more about this powerful marketing program. Go to www.RuthlessMarketing.com right now and read all about it.

Then you can go to the website address below and get a great FREE Gift that can help you make even more money!

www.ingramcontent.com/pod-product-compliance
Lightning Source LLC
Chambersburg PA
CBHW032012190326
41520CB00007B/449